Snake and the Birds

Written by Jill Eggleton

Illustrated by Stella Yang

The animals in the book

Snake

the birds

The place in the book

Snake saw a bird in a nest.

"Eggs," he said.
"Eggs will be in that nest.
And I'm hungry for eggs."

So Snake went...

slither, slither, slither

up the tree.

And…

slither, slither, slither

up to the nest.

"Can I get into your nest?" said Snake.

"No," said the bird.
"I can't have a snake in my nest."

"Can you make me a nest then?" said Snake.
"I have no beak like you."

6

Snake's tongue went...

flick, **flick,** **flick.**

"I can do that," he said.

So the bird went away to make Snake a nest.

Snake was going...

slither, slither, slither

up the next tree.

A bird was sitting in her nest.

Snake went...

slither, slither, slither

up to the nest.

10

"Can you get me a worm?" he said to the bird.

"No," said the bird.
"I'm sitting on my eggs."

Snake will...

get in the nest?

eat the bird?

Snake's tongue went...

flick, flick, flick.

"I'm very hungry," he said.
"I can't get worms.
I have no beak like you."

"OK," said the bird.
"But you'll have to look after my eggs."

"I can do that," said Snake.

So the bird went
to get Snake a worm.
When she came back,
her eggs were gone
and so was Snake.

Snake was sleeping in the grass.
But...

Snake woke up.

He saw wings.

He saw eyes.

He saw claws.

He saw beaks.

And the beaks were going

TAP,

TAP,

TAP,

all over him!

"**Stop!**" said Snake.

But the birds said,
"**You took our eggs!
You took our eggs!
You took our eggs!**"

The birds are...?

Snake took off.

Slither, slither, slither,

slither, slither, slither,

over the ground and into a hole.

And the birds didn't see Snake again.

The End

An action/consequence chart

Snake goes up to
the nest.

Bird goes away.

Bird goes away.

Snake eats the eggs.

Snake eats the eggs.

Bird tells the other birds.

Bird tells the other birds.

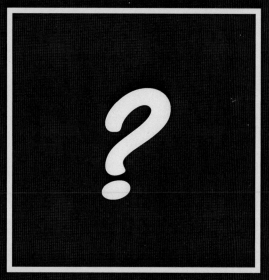

Word Bank

beak

nest

eggs

tongue

grass

worm